D1274708

Showtime Book

Helen Skillicorn

GROLIER

90 Old Sherman Turnpike
Danbury, CT 06816

Published 2003 by Grolier
90 Old Sherman Turnpike
Danbury, CT 06816
A Division of Scholastic Library Publishing

Set ISBN: 0-7172-5760-6
Volume ISBN: 0-7172-5767-3

For information address the publisher:
Grolier, 90 Old Sherman Turnpike, Danbury, CT 06816

Library of Congress Cataloging-in-Publication Data

Crafts for kids.
p. cm.
Includes indexes.
Contents: [1] Backyard book—[2] Bedroom book—[3] Vacation book—[4] World book—[5] Winter holiday book—[6] Back-to-school book—[7] Showtime book—[8] Bead book—[9] Valentine book—[10] Dolls and bears book—[11] Ghostly book —[12] Games book—[13] Birthday book—[14] Fancy dress book—[15] Friendship book—[16] Myths and tales book.
ISBN 0-7172-5760-6 (set : alk. paper)
1. Handicraft—Juvenile literature. 2. Cookery—Juvenile literature. 3. Games—Juvenile literature. [1. Handicraft.] I. Grolier Incorporated.

TT160 .C747 2003
745.5—dc21

2002026405

For The Brown Reference Group plc.
Craftperson: Helen Skillicorn
Project Editor: Jane Scarsbrook
Designer: Joan Curtis
Photography: Martin Norris
Design Manager: Lynne Ross
Managing Editor: Bridget Giles
Editorial Director: Lindsey Lowe

Printed and bound in Singapore

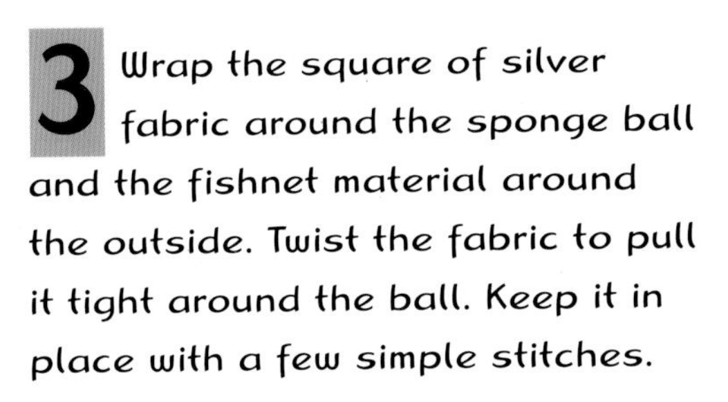

3 Wrap the square of silver fabric around the sponge ball and the fishnet material around the outside. Twist the fabric to pull it tight around the ball. Keep it in place with a few simple stitches.

4 Ask an adult to cut the cardboard roll down to the length you want. Tape silver fabric to the roll, wrap it around, and glue it in place to hide the tape. Tuck spare fabric into the roll at the top and bottom.

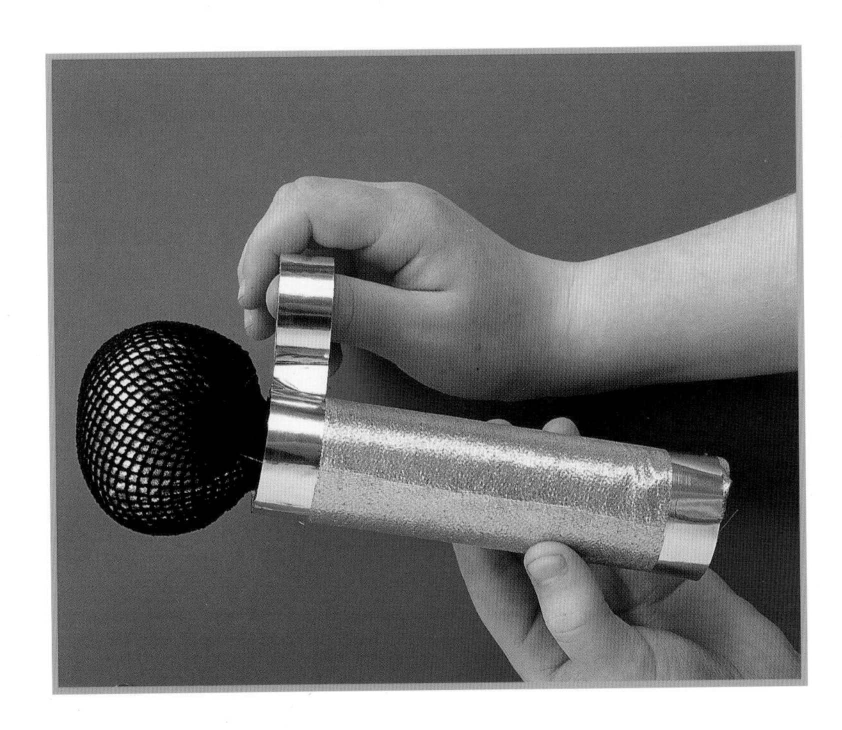

5 Dab glue onto the fabric "neck" of the microphone head, and push it into the silver roll. Let the glue dry. Wind silver tape around the top and bottom of the microphone handle for a smart finish.

6 To add a short wire, cut out a small disk of cardboard that fits inside the end of the handle. Cover it with silver tape. Ask an adult to make a hole in the middle of the disk using a darning needle. Push a short piece of shoelace through the hole, and wind silver tape around the other end of the wire. Glue the disk into the end of the microphone.

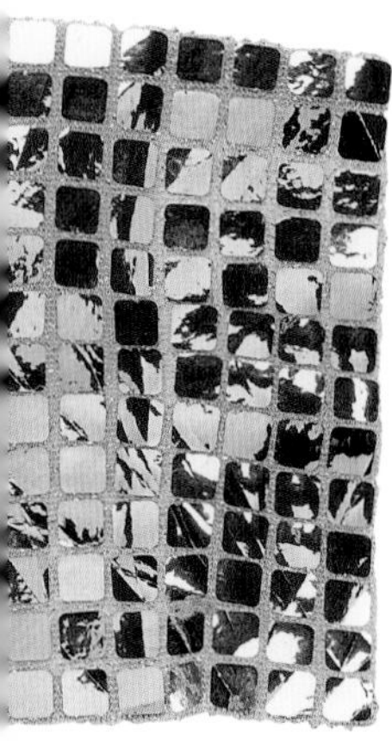

Space pod

This is a cool moon craft for the space puppets you made on page 8. Use the curtain to hide your hand so you can make the astronaut appear in a porthole and aliens pop up through the pod door.

YOU WILL NEED

- small paper bowl
- two paper plates
- silvery fabric
- ribbed cardboard
- silver spray paint
- sequin waste from a craft shop
- scissors
- glue
- masking tape
- newspaper
- strong wire
- 5 metal washers
- shiny fabric for curtain

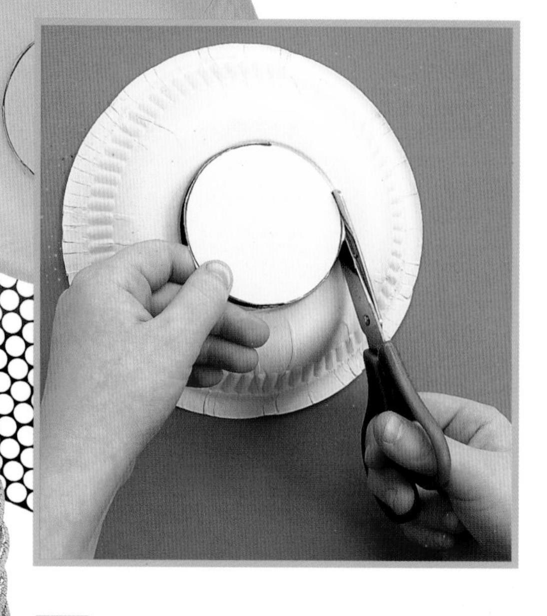

1 First make the roof of the space pod with a trapdoor. Take a paper bowl, and cut out the circular base, but don't cut all the way around.

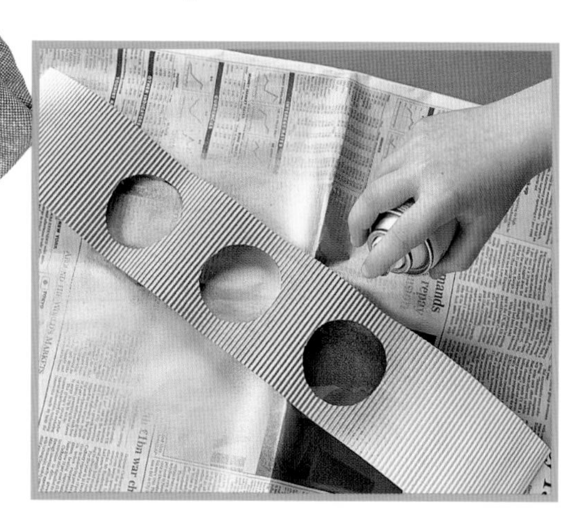

2 Cut a strip of ribbed cardboard about 4in (10cm) wide and long enough to wrap around the rim of the paper bowl. Draw three circles for portholes, and cut them out. Now ask an adult to cover the table with newspaper so you can spray the cardboard strip silver. Spray the bowl roof, too.

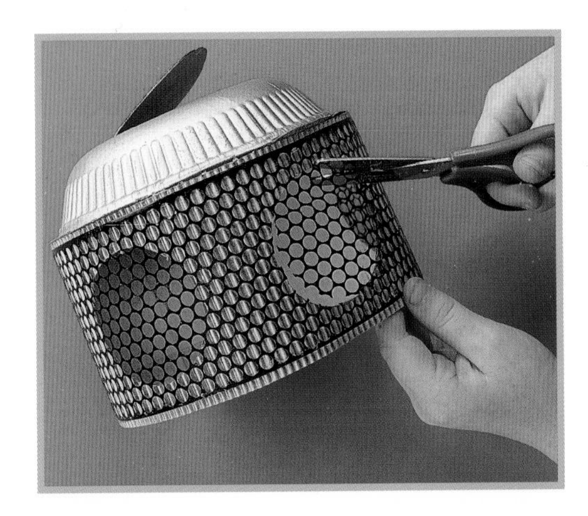

3 Glue the cardboard strip to the rim of the bowl. Let the glue dry. Now cut a strip of sequin waste to cover the cardboard strip. Glue it down, and cut out circles over the portholes—but don't cut out complete circles; leave a bit uncut at the top to make porthole flaps.

When you use spray paint, cover the table with newspaper, and keep the windows open. You may find it easier to do your spray painting outside.

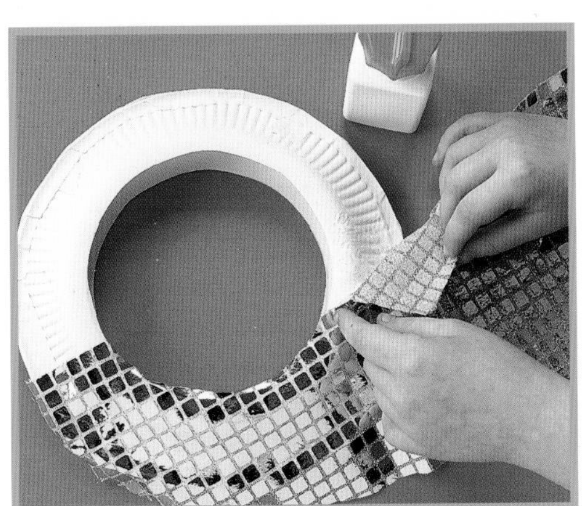

4 To make the base of the pod, slot two paper plates together, and cut out a circle from the center of both plates. To get the size of the circle right, draw around the pod. Turn one plate over, and glue the two plates together around the rims. Let dry. Decorate the pod base by gluing on pieces of silvery fabric.

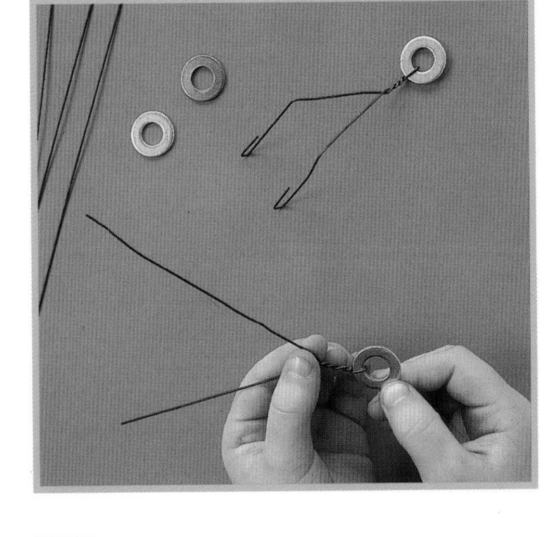

5 To make a pod foot, take a piece of wire 8in (20cm) long. Poke it through a metal washer, and twist the two wire ends. Make a bend in both ends halfway along. Now bend the two wire tips to make hooks. Make 5 pod feet in this way.

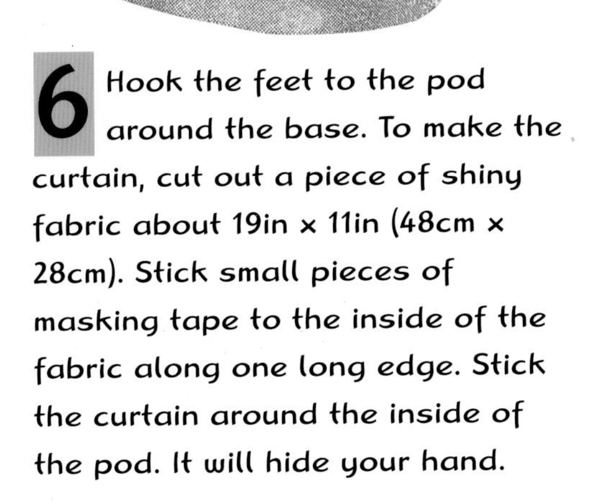

6 Hook the feet to the pod around the base. To make the curtain, cut out a piece of shiny fabric about 19in x 11in (48cm x 28cm). Stick small pieces of masking tape to the inside of the fabric along one long edge. Stick the curtain around the inside of the pod. It will hide your hand.

Dopey dog

Make these cuddly hand puppets from old socks! Follow the steps to make a dog with floppy ears from a brown sock, or try making a giraffe out of a yellow sock with buttons sewn on for horns.

YOU WILL NEED

- cardboard
- potato
- light brown paint
- adult's brown sock
- red felt
- needle and thread
- brown fake fur
- pink felt
- fabric glue
- paper
- scissors
- two paper beads
- black felt-tip pen
- orange pipe cleaner
- yellow wool
- pink pompom

1 Push a piece of cardboard into a sock to keep it flat. Ask an adult to cut a round stamp out of a potato. Dip the potato stamp into light brown paint, and cover the foot of the sock with spot stamps.

Ask an adult to cut out a potato stamp. Make a round stamp for the dog and a square stamp for the giraffe.

3 Draw an ear shape onto paper, and cut it out. Pin the paper pattern onto pink felt, and cut around the pattern. Make two pink felt ears in this way—they are the insides of the dog's ears. Glue the pink felt pieces to the underside of a piece of brown fake fur. Cut out the furry ears.

2 Cut a big tongue shape out of red felt. Sew it onto the sock about 2in (5cm) from the toe on one side.

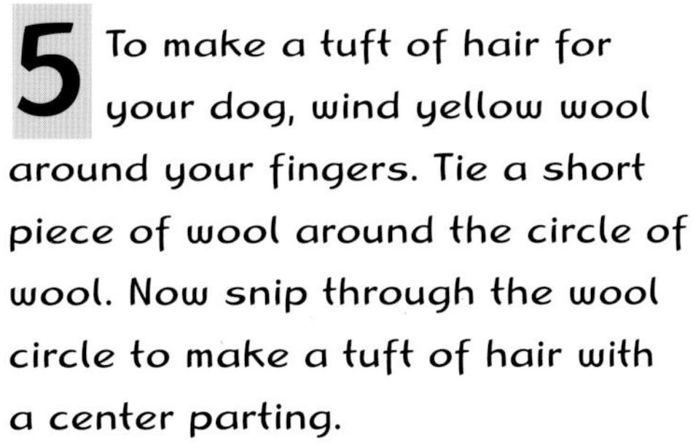

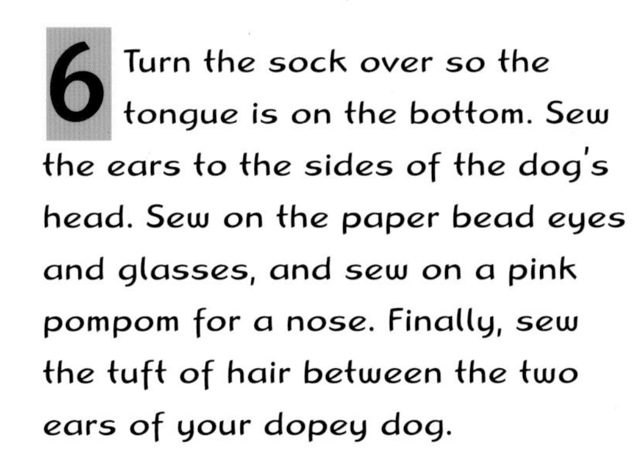

4 To make the eyes, draw pupils onto two paper beads using a black felt-tip pen. Make a pair of glasses by twisting a pipe cleaner into the shape shown above.

5 To make a tuft of hair for your dog, wind yellow wool around your fingers. Tie a short piece of wool around the circle of wool. Now snip through the wool circle to make a tuft of hair with a center parting.

6 Turn the sock over so the tongue is on the bottom. Sew the ears to the sides of the dog's head. Sew on the paper bead eyes and glasses, and sew on a pink pompom for a nose. Finally, sew the tuft of hair between the two ears of your dopey dog.

Model theater

This beautiful theater has a curtain to open and close the show. Ask an adult to cut out the pieces you need to build your theater.

YOU WILL NEED

- mounting board
- craft knife
- cutting mat
- metal ruler
- strong glue
- gold glitter pen
- gold paint pen
- star stickers

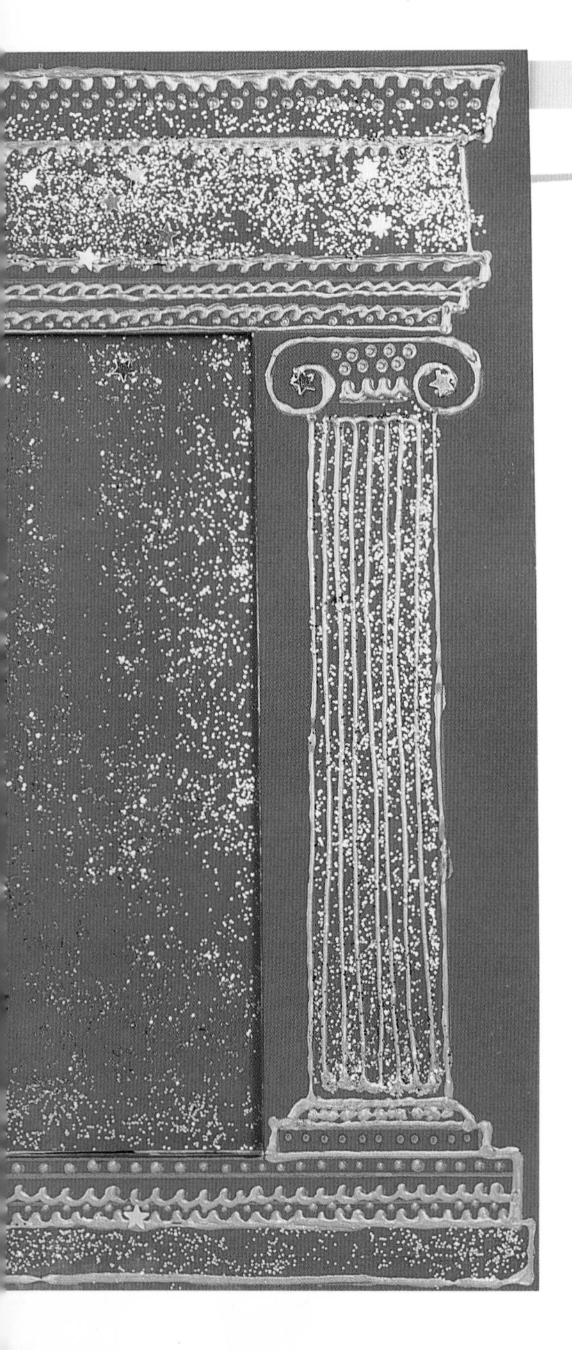

1 First ask an adult to cut out three pieces of mounting board each 12½in x 10in (32cm x 25cm). They will be: the stage floor, the back wall, and the front arch. Ask an adult to cut out a window from one piece to make the front arch. The window should measure 8in x 6¾in (20cm x 17cm) and be 2¼in (6cm) from the top and the two sides, and 1in (2.5cm) from the bottom.

2 Now you have the front arch of your theater. Decorate it by using a gold paint pen to draw on pillars with curly tops.

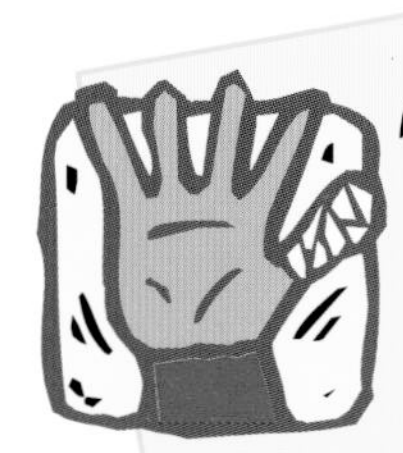

Ask an adult to cut the mounting board using a craft knife and a cutting mat.

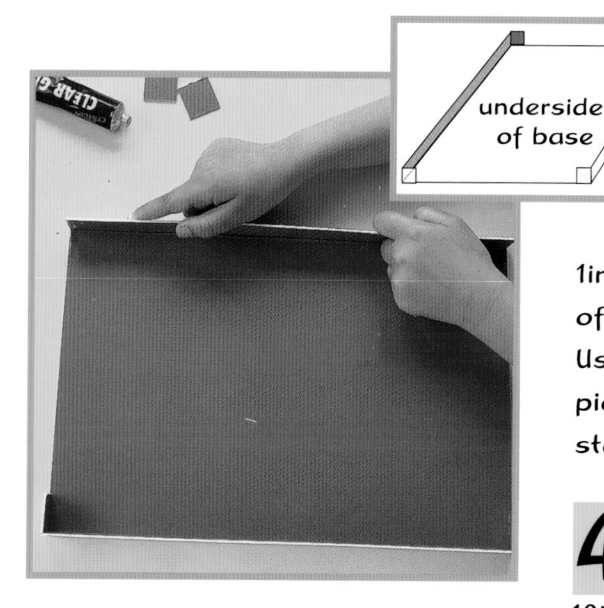

3 To make the base of the theater, ask an adult to cut out two strips of board 12½in x 1in (32cm x 2.5cm) and four squares of board 1in x 1in (2.5cm x 2.5cm). Use strong, clear glue to stick the pieces to the underside of the stage floor as shown.

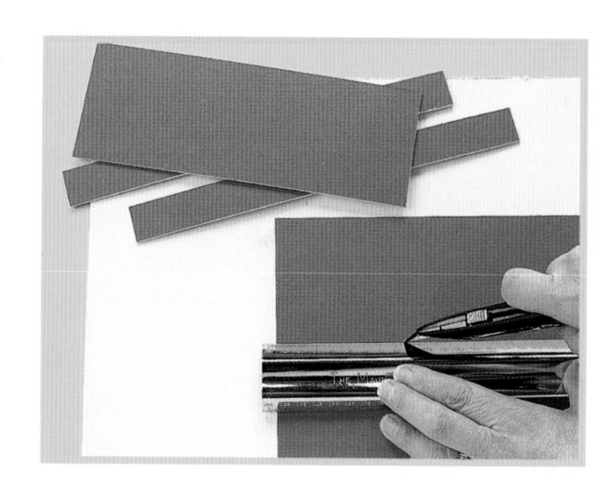

4 To make the side walls of the theater, ask an adult to cut out two pieces of board 3in x 9in (8cm x 22cm) and two strips of board 10in x 1in (25cm x 2.5cm). Glue a thin strip along the top of a fat strip to make a "T" shape—this is a side wall.

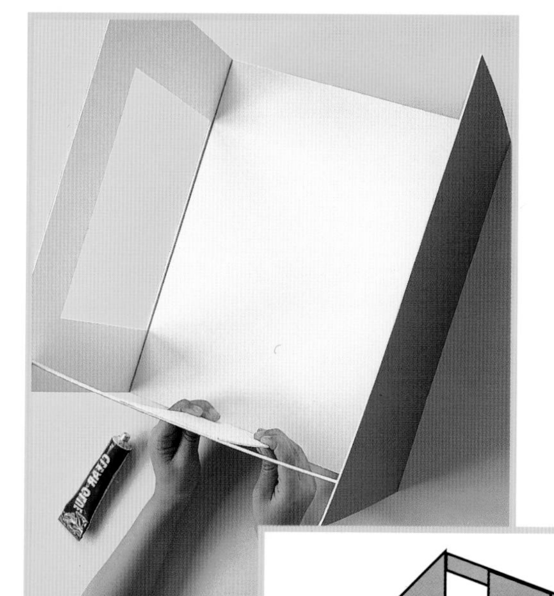

5 To put the theater together, glue the front archway and the back wall to the theater base. Now put the side walls in place, and glue them where they meet the stage floor, the front arch, and the back wall of the theater.

6 To make a curtain, cut out a piece of red cardboard 9in x 10in (22cm x 25cm). Glue a thin strip of cardboard along the top so you can hang the curtain on the side walls of the theater. Decorate the curtain with glitter glue (rubbed in with your finger) and gold star stickers.

Theater scenery

Here are some clever ideas you can try out to make a scene for your model theater. Try making pieces that stand on the stage, like this fairytale castle, or pieces that hang from above, like the fluffy white clouds.

YOU WILL NEED

- white cushion stuffing or cotton wool
- thin wire
- white cardboard
- scissors
- sky-patterned wrapping paper
- silver cardboard
- shiny silver, blue, and red paper
- scissors
- pencil
- small branches for trees
- glue
- silver paint
- air-drying clay

1 Cut out a piece of shiny wrapping paper 12½in x 10in (32cm x 25cm), and lay it on the stage floor of the theater. Cut out a strip of patterned paper to make a royal carpet. It will lead up to the door of the castle.

2 To make a sky backdrop, use the model theater curtain from page 17. Cover the back with sky-patterned wrapping paper, or draw sky and clouds onto paper, and stick it on. Hang the backdrop at the back of the theater.

3 Tear off a piece of cushion stuffing or cotton wool to make a cloud. Push a piece of thin wire through the cloud, and bend the two wire ends to make hooks. Cut out a strip of cardboard long enough to stretch across the theater, and rest it on the side walls. Hook on the clouds.

5 Draw a castle onto silver cardboard—you can copy our design. Push your scissors through the cardboard at the top of the pointed door, and cut down the middle line. Then cut a little way down the curved sides so that you can fold open the castle doors.

4 To make a tree, push a small branch into a chunk of air-drying clay with a flat base. Let the clay harden. Make two trees for either side of the stage. Paint or spray the trees silver. Glue on leaves made from silver paper.

6 Cut out pointed roofs from blue shiny paper, and stick them on. Cut out windows and a flag, too. Cover the insides of the doors with shiny paper—you will see them when the doors are open.

7 Cut out two right-angled triangles (see picture on the right) from cardboard, and glue them onto the back of the castle at the bottom so the castle stands up.

Theater princess

Now that you've made a theater and set the scene, it's time to put on a play. We've made a king, a princess, and a wicked wizard to appear on our stage, but you can make any characters you like.

YOU WILL NEED

- thin white cardboard
- pencil
- compass
- mounting board
- ruler
- glue
- scissors
- wrapping paper
- white pipe cleaner
- felt-tip pens
- shiny paper and ribbon for the hat
- gold thread
- yellow embroidery thread
- paper bead
- needle and thread
- velcro strips
- strong white cardboard

1 To make the body, draw a semicircle with a 5in (12.5cm) diameter onto white cardboard. You can do so by using a compass and placing the compass needle on the edge of the cardboard, or draw around a bowl. Now draw a small circle with a 1in (2.5cm) diameter on mounting board. Cut it out.

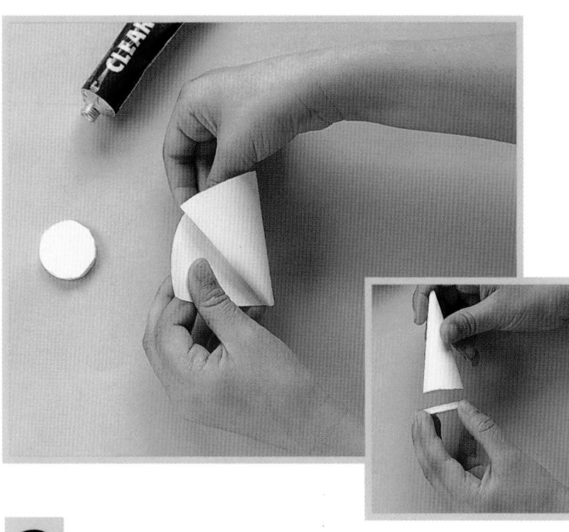

2 Make a cone shape from the semicircle, and adjust it so that the base of the cone is the same size as the circle of mounting board. Stick down the cone. Glue the mounting board base to the cone.

Ask an adult to help you use a sharp needle and to help you use a compass.

3 To make the dress, cut out a semicircle of wrapping paper, and glue it around the cone.

4 To make arms with flared sleeves, cut a shape out of wrapping paper like the one in the picture on the right. Bend the ends of a pipe cleaner to make hands. Fold the paper over the stem, and glue it down. Glue the arms to the back of the princess's body.

5 Glue a paper bead onto the point of the cone to make the head. Make a cone out of shiny paper for the hat, and glue ribbon to the top. Cut lengths of thread to make hair, and glue them to the top of the princess's head. Wind gold thread around the hair to make plaits, and draw a face.

6 Cut a strip of strong white cardboard about 10in (25cm) long and 1in (2.5cm) wide. Stick on a square of velcro (the loopy part) to one end of the strip. Stick a square of velcro (the hooked part) to the base of the princess. Now you can move her around the stage in your fairytale play.

Endless handkerchief

This is a simple trick for a beginner magician. Tuck the handkerchief into the pocket of the vest on page 24, or make a trick pocket in an old pair of trousers. When you give the handkerchief a tug, an endless, colorful stream spills out.

YOU WILL NEED

- silky or shiny fabric in three colors
- needle and thread
- pinking shears
- scissors
- ruler
- chalk
- old pair of trousers

1 Cut a strip of shiny fabric 6in (15cm) wide. The shiny fabric will make it easier to pull the handkerchief out of your pocket with a smooth flourish! Make a mark every 6in (15cm) along both long edges using chalk.

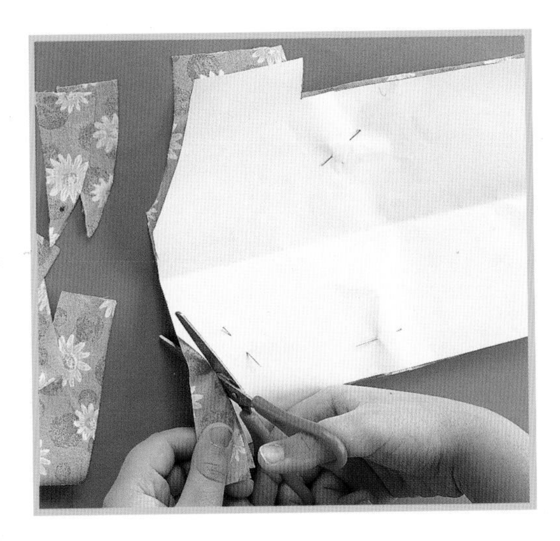

3 Trace the dress half pattern on page 30. Transfer it onto folded paper, lining up the center of the pattern with the fold. Cut out the paper pattern, and pin it to the flowery fabric. Cut out the dress. Use the paper pattern to cut out a second dress shape.

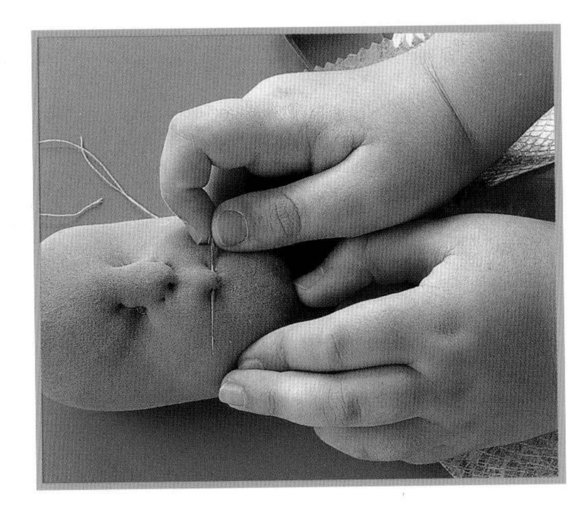

6 To put the doll together glue the neck of the dress around the cardboard roll. Glue the hands to the insides of the sleeves, and pop on her vest. Cut a fringed hem for the vest. To make the doll's features, sew simple stitches into the squashy head.

4 Use pinking shears to cut a zigzag hem for the dress. Glue the front and the back of the dress together along the sides and shoulders. Now trace the vest back pattern, and use it to cut out the shape in mock-snakeskin fabric. Trace the vest front pattern, and use it to cut out two flaps of mock snakeskin. Glue the vest fronts to the vest back at the sides and shoulders.

7 To make long, hippy hair, wind wool around a stiff piece of cardboard. Tie the wool at the top, and cut it at the bottom.

5 Cut out two hands from brown craft foam. You can glue the little finger and the ring finger of one hand to the thumb to make a "peace sign." Cut out shades from pink cardboard.

Ask an adult to help you use a sharp needle.

Peacock mask

This beautiful carnival mask is made from papier-mâché. You will need to let the mask dry overnight and go on with this project the next day.

YOU WILL NEED

- balloon
- masking tape
- small bowl
- newspaper
- scissors
- wallpaper paste (the type without fungicide)
- brush for glue
- petroleum jelly
- thin cardboard
- pencil
- dark blue, light blue, yellow, and gold acrylic paint
- paintbrush
- glue
- feathers
- sequins
- ribbon

1 Blow up a balloon. To keep the balloon still, put it in a small bowl and stick it in place with masking tape. Smear petroleum jelly over the balloon—cover an area big enough to mask the top half of your face down to your nose and back to your ears.

2 Mix up a bowl of wallpaper paste following the instructions on the package. Tear up strips of newspaper, and paint the greased balloon with glue. Paste on strips of newspaper using a brush or your fingers. Paste on seven layers. For each layer paste the strips on in a different direction. That will help you cover the balloon evenly.

3 Let the papier-mâché balloon dry overnight in a warm place. When it is dry, pop the balloon. Cut out a half-mask shape. Draw on eyes and a triangle at the bottom for your nose. Cut them out.

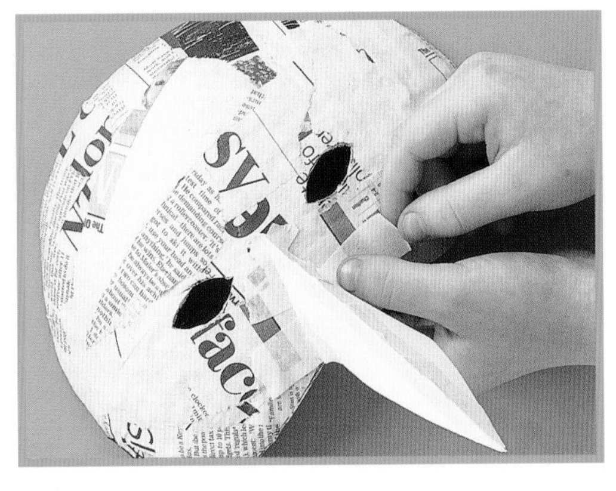

4 Fold a piece of white cardboard in half, and draw on a beak. Cut it out so you have two beak shapes. Use masking tape to stick the curved edges together to make the beak. Tape the beak onto the mask over the nose triangle. Paste the beak with two or three layers of papier-mâché. Let it dry.

5 Paint the mask dark blue, and then paint the eye area gold.

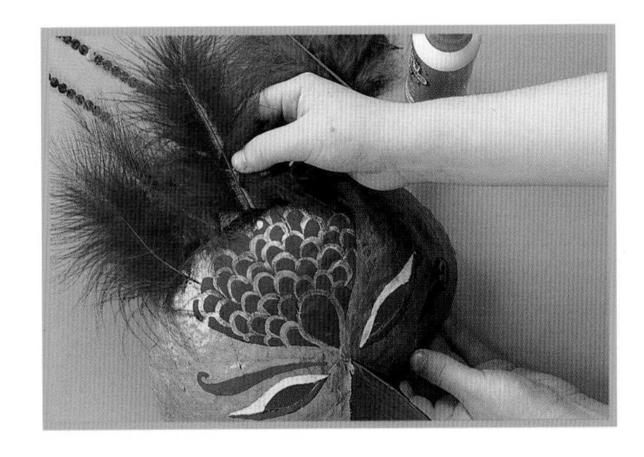

6 Draw a feather pattern onto the forehead with a marker pen. Paint the top feathers light blue, and go over the feather pattern with gold paint. Line the eyes with blue and yellow paint. Tape feathers to the inside of the mask at the top, and decorate with sequins. Ask an adult to make a hole on either side of the mask using scissors. Thread ribbon through the holes so you can tie the mask around your head.

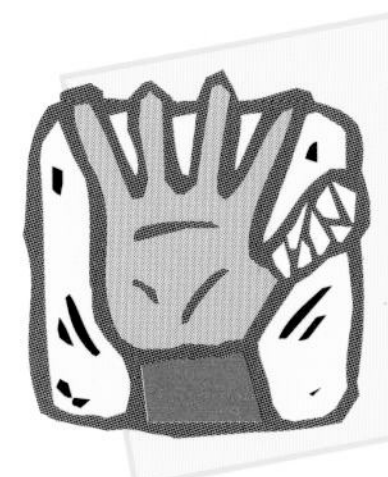

Ask an adult to make two holes in the mask for the ribbons.

Patterns

Here are the patterns you will need to make some of the projects. To find out how to make a pattern, follow the instructions on page 5.

Some of the patterns are half patterns. To find out how to make a whole pattern, read the instructions for the project.

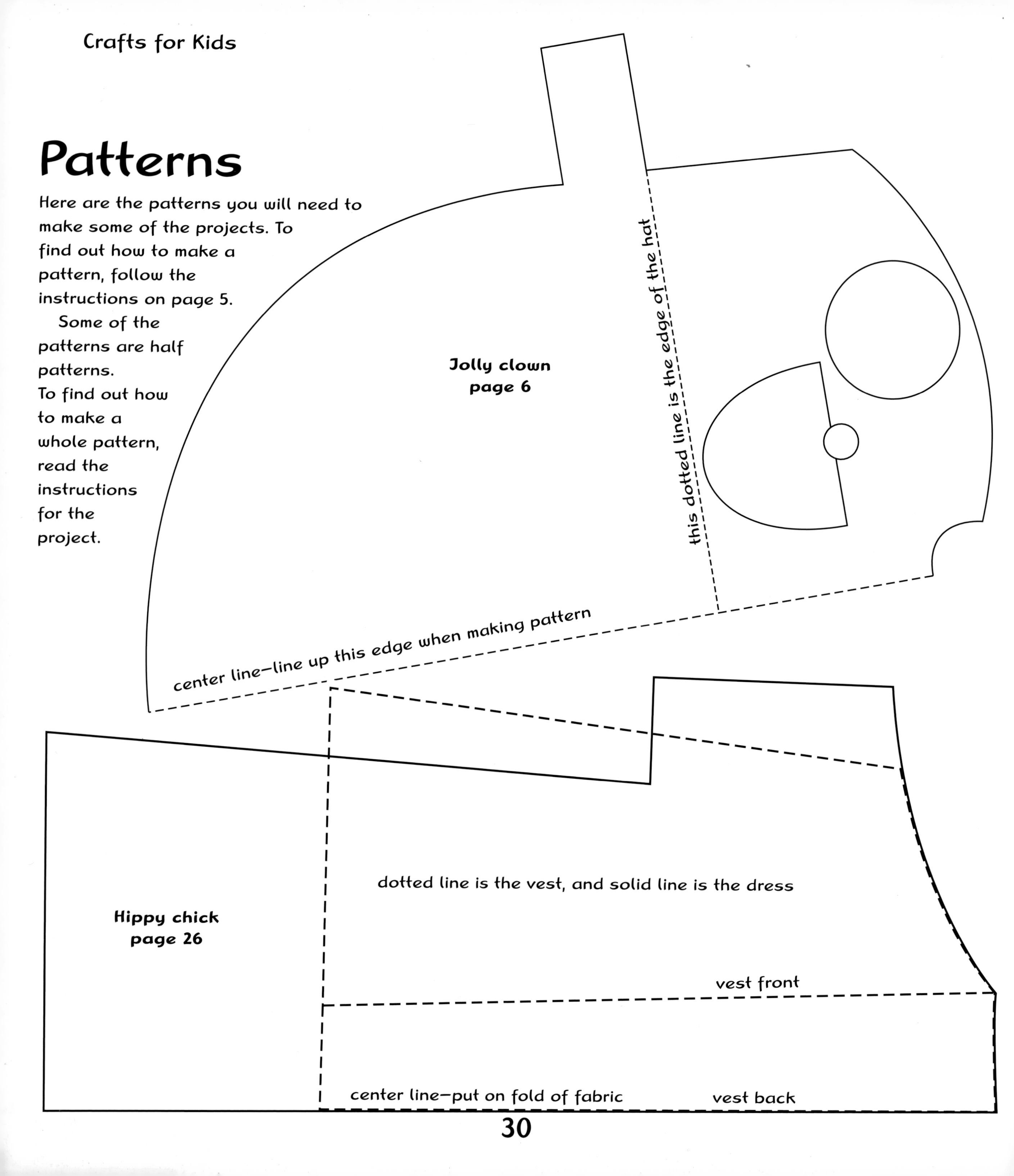

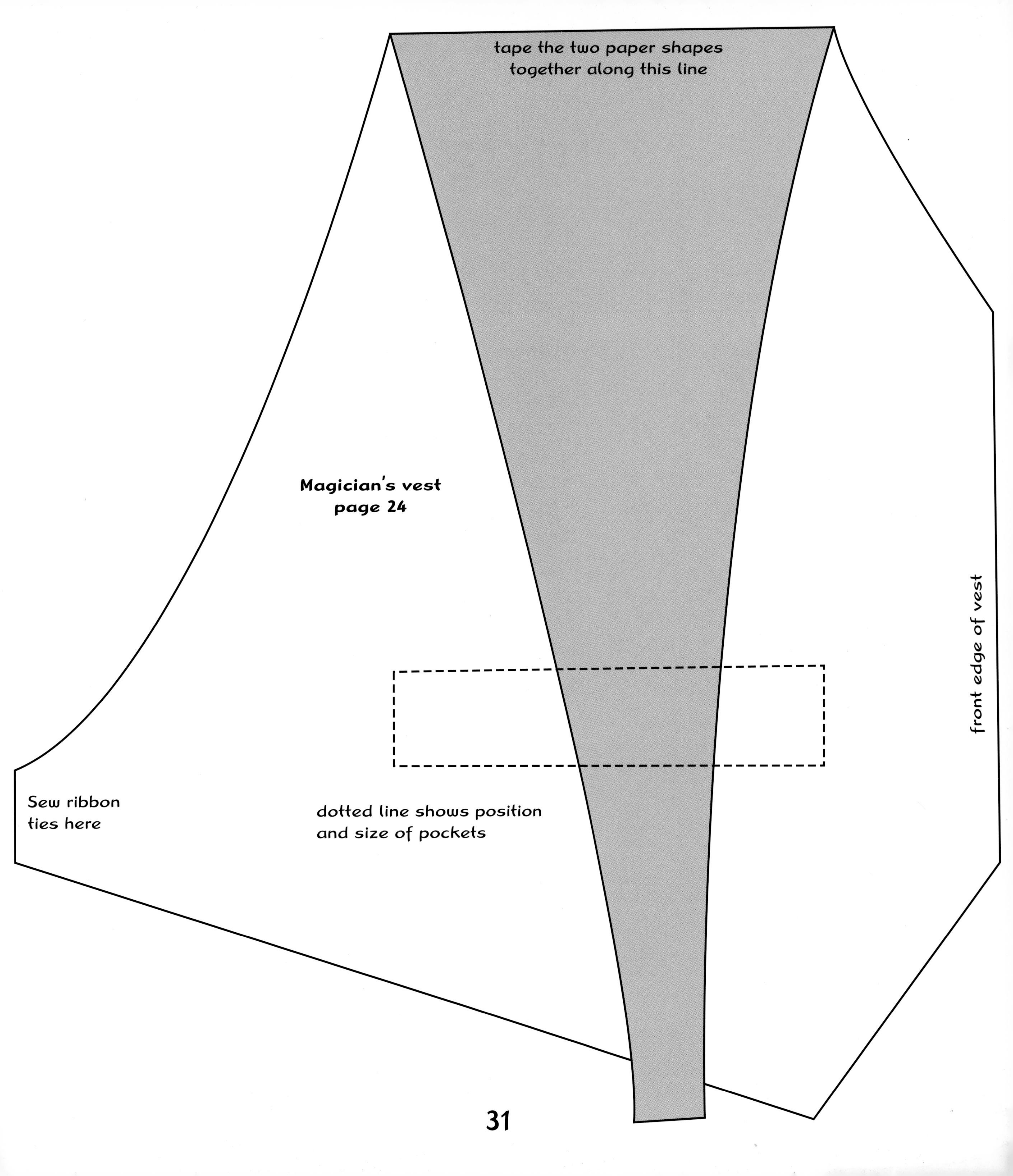
tape the two paper shapes
together along this line
Magician's vest
page 24
front edge of vest
Sew ribbon
ties here
dotted line shows position
and size of pockets

Index